I0766335

Letters & Lyrics

CONTENTS OF THE HEART

Expressions of A Single Woman, Part II

NICHELLE HODGE

Dedication

This book is for all those who still believe in love.

I love you, and there is nothing you can do about it!

Contents From My Heart

A collection of writings candidly expressed about:

FAITH - FAMILY - FANCY

Faith

Journey of a Lifetime

The story of how I came to Christ was a bonus feature of a previously published book, entitled *Dating without Discrimination—Expressions of A Single Woman*... The material shared was about the character encountered while dating or collecting data of the opposite sex—a heterosexual male—regardless of race, religion, economic status, and social class. The result of those lessons was to reestablish my relationship with Christ. For it is in this, the most important of relationships, that I am reminded of my value, worth, and purpose.

What I have to say now about the subject of faith is that it is still a precious gift, which needs to be unwrapped, and utilized daily—in bold, courageous, and practical ways. It's not a one-size fits-all present. However, I believe that we all have enough of it that can be used to better our lives and those around us.

Faith is an abundant resource given to us by God to accomplish what fear says we cannot do. It is said that faith is the opposite of fear. Faith not only believes in what's invisible; it works together with wisdom and knowledge to make the invisible tangible.

Faith is also needed to get you through every stage of life. The levels of it may vary, but it is a necessity to help accomplish anything of lasting value. Besides, the word of God says that without faith, it is impossible to please Him—see *Hebrews 11:6*.

By faith, even though I had some level of fear, remarkable things have been accomplished in my life. Generational curses have been broken! Lives have changed for the better! Fruit has grown and reproduced because of the faith I used. I also have enough faith to believe that there is more left for me to do, to the glory of God here on earth.

Here are a few memories from my faith files. To God be the glory!

Often, I intentionally take inventory of my attitude and gratitude, being careful not to be so self-observed or expressing an entitlement mentality.

There have been seasons in my life where I needed help for the necessities of life, like food, clothing, and shelter. There was not time to be prideful and act as if I had it all together. That would only make matters worse. When I was a young single parent, it was no longer about me. I had to do what needed to be done, so my son could have a better quality of life.

I remember applying for government assistance for food and health care benefits. The help would be temporary because I had a plan to be more stabilized. Also, I wanted to be more of a giver to others in need. For the help of so many and with a humble heart, thank you! You were instruments used to answer prayers.

There are two distinct occasions in my life when I was without anything other than what was in my possession, which meant the clothes that I had on my back. I have had to stay in shelters, cars, hallways, and on people's floors. All temporary, yet still humbling.

The first time was a weekend that I will never forget… I was out visiting a friend for the day and planned to hang out for the rest of the weekend, so I went back to where I was staying at the time. In a matter of minutes, so many things took place, and there were intense, escalated, and severe consequences. The results were that everything that I owned was packed into garbage bags and thrown away. To be on the receiving end of another person's hatred could leave one bitter and vengeful. However, my life was spared, and God has restored my life many times over.

The second time was when I graduated from high school. My mother and twin sister came to celebrate with me. I had no idea of what trial I would encounter once I left the United States.

After traveling on a one-way ticket to the British Virgin Islands, I was in shock. The ride from West End to Brewer's Bay was beautiful. The weather was perfect. When the taxi got to our destination, I expected a house to live in. Yet, my mother took her key and unlocked the tent. A real camping tent! I did not know how to react. My mother explained that the situation was temporary, and she believed that God was going to turn things around. In the meantime, we endured the season of lack in a very humble way. To this day, it is a reminder to not take anything or anyone for granted.

As my mother exhibited her faith, mine began to grow, too. I was angry with God about what He allowed us to go through. It felt cruel and unfair. I did not understand. I forgot to be thankful for what He was doing. He provided shelter, even though it looked different. He protected us. He even gave us the luxury of living rent-free, with a beach just steps away from the tent.

The Lord does have a profound sense of humor. By faith, which had been truly tested by fire, He blessed me with my first house. Hallelujah! For me, it was like Joseph being released from prison to the palace. All the while, God was with him.

That is my testimony! No matter what was allowed to take place in my life—losing it all, to now having more than enough—God has been with me. He is still with me and will always be with me!

I have not only the faith to believe, but also the courage to do something with that faith. This is a faith walk, and until my work here on earth is complete, I'm going to keep on walking! Amen!

Family

Redefined

Biologically, I have two siblings: my mother's firstborn and eldest daughter of three-and-a-half years, and a twin sister. I am the last-born twin by nineteen minutes.

My mother made sure to encourage my twin sister and I to have our own identity. While we shared time and space, she knew that we were both unique, with our own set of gifts and personalities.

To say that my siblings and I did not have challenges growing up would not be honest. We have had highs, lows, the good, the bad, the pretty, and the ugly. We shared some disagreements, but also laughter, and tears. Now as adults, we choose to live our lives separately from each other. At the present, we reside in the same state, but we are worlds apart.

I have learned that my siblings, at most times, are my relatives. I mean no harm when I share this. We have similar features, ways, and experiences... Hence, the word "relate."

Family, however, after the passing of our mother, has taken on a whole new meaning for me. It was at her funeral that I began to understand the difference.

Matthew 12:50 NKJV - **"For whoever does the will of My Father who is in Heaven, he is my brother, and sister, and mother."**

My mother was the firstborn on both sides of her family, which makes us the oldest of the grandchildren and nieces. However, my mother was not as close in relation to her siblings. We knew of our grandparents, aunts, uncles, and cousins, but we were not close to creating intimate relationships.

The closest relationships are with people to whom I am not biologically related.

Unfortunately, I did not get a chance to meet my maternal grandmother. She passed prematurely while we were children. I remember my mother grieving her loss, but not understanding that kind of pain.

My grandmother, not by heritage, is from Alabama. She lived most of her life in Massachusetts. She is still content living there and being a blessing to the rest of her family. She is one of the first women whom my mother met when she came to the States. She is a woman of faith and is loving to all who know her. She never meets a stranger. She is giving and graceful.

Grandma Bettye—you taught me that love judges less and forgives more. Thank you for the love you have shown me and Jeremiah over the years as if we were your own. May God continue to bless you and keep you. I love you!

I believe my mother has at least six living sisters and two brothers, which are my aunts and uncles. They live in the Caribbean and in the States. We did not grow up getting to see them often as children, teenagers, or young adults.

Again, I knew of them, but did not get to know them in a close way. Every now and again, we will send a greeting, then get back to living our distant and separate lives. Distance, for me, is not what makes my heart grow fonder—it makes it fainter. No love lost.

The Lord has allowed my family to grow over the years. I have also done my part to get to know people and build community.

I am wonderfully blessed to have relationships with people who I have known for many years: Mornel, who taught me about class and standards; Sherry, who taught me about faithfulness; and Julian, who taught me about how longsuffering means to suffer long. I truly thank God for you. You have been my friends for decades and have watched me grow into the woman that I am today. You have checked, watered, cried, and laughed with me. Please know that you are loved and appreciated.

My cousin and sister-friends: Michelle, who taught me about walking consistently in my purpose; Stephanie, who taught me to have a variety in relationships; Denise, who taught me about being a better money manager; and others have taught me to love within the proper boundaries, treat them with gentle care, kindness, and patience. Thank you for your accountability, boldness, and courage. You, too, have been a part of the growth of my faith, and I am better because of your godly examples and influences.

Proverbs 18:24a NKJV - "**A man who has friends must himself be friendly...**"

My prayer is that I have also been and continue to be a friendly, kind, giving, loving, and caring person to each of you. My prayer for you all is that you continue to grow in the grace, wisdom, favor, and love of God all the days of your lives. May you be in good health and prosper, even as your soul prospers. Many more blessings upon you and your loved ones. In the name of Jesus! Amen.

Expressions of Family

Friends... that stick closer than a brother or sister
Are... not judgmental but will tell you like it is.
Made... to be different, even though you have similarities.
In... spite of what they may think, do they accept you as you are?
Life... Live it! Don't just exist.
Yet... you may not share the same blood; you are still a part of my family.

Fancy

Expressions of A Single Woman

Part II

The "Expressions" that follow are thoughts from my heart in the form of lessons learned, poetry, short stories, and statements. While I actively practice being more careful with guarding my heart, it is a delight when I can share some of the intimate parts of it with others.

Expressions To a Soldier

You slid into my DM. You were on your way to travel on another tour. The last one. You wanted to return home to your family and start a new life. You were interested in making me a part of your life.

As I have done in times past, throwing caution to the wind, I engaged in cyber conversation turned wishful love affair with you that was fun and refreshing. The kind of elementary love you had with a crush in high school. I was giddy, smiling like a schoolchild.

Oops! I did it again!

I lowered the shield that was supposed to be guarding my heart. The helmet that was meant to protect my mind was now sitting next to me in the chair, while my feet were propped up, as if I did not have a care in the world.

We talked about present-day life and the possibility of what a future, our future, could look like if we were willing to put in the work.

You wasted no time initiating and extending an invitation to that possibility. You said that you did not want to waste time or risk the chance of getting hurt. You wanted honesty from the beginning. How ironic.

Without hesitation, I accepted the offer. The risk-taking, loyal to a fault, and, at times, foolish lover that I am—I committed to a hopeful "maybe."

The days that passed between us were surreal. You called me all the "baby," "honey," "sweetheart," "darlings." Your words were sweet like honey. Oh, how I was not prepared for the sting that was soon to follow.

Something was off! While I felt it, I did not dismiss it, and I did not pay closer attention to the shift like I really needed to.

First, you were working late and unable to communicate for long. I chalked that up to distance and being in different time zones. "He is working, girl!" "Do not take it personal!" The sidebar conversations I had with myself to feel less anxious.

Then, just like that... You were more accessible. You were checking in with me more frequently. Not that I did not appreciate the attentiveness, but it was not the norm that I had become accustomed to.

The tone changed, like I was having a conversation with a completely different person. This time, my antennae were up! The normal formalities were shared between us, but there was no "love" present.

I had to talk myself back right. Finally, in my right mind, I said, "Here it comes!" and "Girl, you have been a fool, but you are not going to be an old fool!"

The story that came up next was not even original. It was not another woman that you threw in my face. It was worse than that: a bold-faced lie!

The lie made me sick. The kind that has you doubled

over the basin. Yet, I knew that I had swallowed a whole lot of vain promises. The only way for me to get better was to face the truth. The truth set me free!

I rose and washed my face. For a moment, I felt shame. I was embarrassed that I was naïve. The moment of weakness could have been more devastating. The loss that I felt did sting.

Yes, I had stumbled, with my heart and eyes wide open, but I did not completely fall. Thank God! God had been gracious to me again... even in my temporary insane state.

The deception was on a different platform, but my anxious actions were the same. Why did I think the results would look any different?

Lord, I repent! I changed my mind. I do not want something or someone so desperately that I am willing to believe a lie!

Dear Soldier, please know that I do not blame you for my failure to exercise discernment. Thank you for being the vessel that was permitted to help me learn, again, the value of contentment. Your actions were a reminder to be more alert.

As I have taught others, everyone who comes into your life is there either to add and multiply, or to distract, subtract, and divide.

You did add me. Your participation in this whole encounter reminded me to practice being less anxious, keep loving me, continue being kind to others, and most importantly, always walk confidently and courageously in my God-given purpose.

Believe me, I meant it when I said, "I love, love!" I believe in real, genuine, authentic love. The kind you give and not just look to receive. True love gives! Intentionally, wholeheartedly, and selflessly.

I had no reason to lie to you. You asked for honesty. I gave that to you.

Remember this, you reap what you sow, more than you sow, and later than you sow.

Expressions on Loving a Black Man

I attempted to give you my all. Yet, you didn't value the gift of me. You made many withdrawals, but the deposits were so few. Instead of returning the love I freely gave in faithful submission, you took it for granted. Disregarded it, even. You admitted that I was only a fantasy. Don't you understand that doesn't flatter me? It's insulting to be kept a secret, and to think that I'd let this be my reality. I'm a rare jewel that has found herself! I refuse to hide my beautiful light just so you can have your cake and eat it, too. I love easy. I love hard. I love long. A fault of my own. I have no regrets of loving you, Black man. I only hoped that you chose me to love, too.

Expressions on Loving Me

I was created from love. Therefore, I am lovable and worthy of receiving genuine love. I am also capable of giving love to others.

John 3:16 says, "**For God so loved the world, that He gave...**"

While love has multiple meanings, I believe the best type of love is agape, unconditional love. The love that Paul describes in detail in *1 Corinthians 13*.

Giving love has never been an issue for me. It is natural. Love, for me, is a verb. An action taken to show what I mean by what I have boldly stated, yet without expecting it to be reciprocated.

The challenge that I have experienced is when it comes to self-love. What I mean by that is that I would not put much thought or effort into loving me. I am practicing this more daily.

Self-love is now more balanced. Eating healthier. Being physically active, so I can move with ease as I get older.

Doing more of the things that I enjoy. Traveling frequently. Laughing often. Explaining myself less. Surrounding myself with people who like, appreciate, and want to spend time with me. Date me, again. Yes! Buy flowers. Dress fancy. Have a nice dinner too.

As I commit to loving all of me, I can continue to love others.

I no longer force relationships, nor do I stay where I am not wanted. If there is resistance, I back all the way off. If there is an invitation to connect, I consider the source and move with discernment.

In my book, *"Dating without Discrimination—Expressions of A Single Woman"*, I wrote about a man whom I really loved. I proclaimed to the world that it was with him that I wanted to spend the rest of my life with. However, I was the only one who felt that way. It was then that I started back on the journey of self-love. There have been distractions along the way. At some point, I sat with depression and bonded with others over trauma.

Yet, now, I enjoy the freedom that I have! I quit acting as though I was a married woman whose attention was divided. I have grown in the respect that I have for myself and demand that others do the same.

I still want forever!

However, while I wait for the Lord to grant me the desires of my heart, I refocus on my purpose and calling. I live boldly and courageously. Apologize when needed, laugh often, and enjoy the liberty that I have even more. Keep showing up and being present. I am a gift, a jewel, meant to shine and be enjoyed! Amen.

Expressions on While I Wait

To My Future Husband—I Am the Destination!
Not a layover. Nor on standby.

Hey, King!
I heard that you were heading my way.
Is it true?
Tell me now, for I've been waiting for you.
A few thoughts from my heart I'd like to share,
If you are willing to lend a listening ear.
Was it the twinkle in my eyes or the thickness of my thighs?
Was it my smile or grin?
Was it the scent of my skin?
Was it the passion of my words,
When I called out to you in the night?
Was it love or lust at first sight?
Do tell, I need to know!
Do I stay or should I go?

Expressions on Accountability

When you sat in the clinic waiting room to abort that child... your own hand destroying your legacy and future generations—did Black Lives Matter?

When you stood at the welfare office to lie about that child's father abandoning you, just to receive benefits you didn't want to work for, letting the "system" be the "other man" that could never be competed with—did Black Lives Matter?

When you chose that career instead of raising those kids who are now disrespectful, rebellious, and in need of saving—did Black Lives Matter?

Yes, there is a real system of racism that includes the slaughter, mass incarceration, racial profiling, economic disparities, and other ungodly, immoral, and foul treatment of the BLACK race... Yet, there's some responsibility in our homes, churches, and communities that we must take for ourselves!!! To heal, some things must be revealed...

Let's talk about that! Amen.

Expressions of Maturity

Finally, as a grown, mature, and learned WHOAman... I understand the importance in seeking wisdom from God as to what role a man is to play in my life. Then, as I exercise that wisdom, we would have to relate to one another to have a relationship. Also, in Amos 3, there is a question asked: *"Can two walk together unless they are agreed?"* That tells me that when two people meet but are moving in opposite directions, it's best to continue moving instead of utilizing time, energy, and resources to grasp for something or someone out of your reach. Most importantly, the individual man led by God will impart wisdom, strength, and substance to my life. Not in the form of material or tangible things, but treasures that will last. I believe that I am determined to no longer settle for or entertain the fleshly desires of humanity. The woman that God created me to be is unique. A gift that is shared with many... but not all will recognize the gift as such. Amen.

Expressions About Being in Your Feelings

You Have a Right... to feel the way you do. Your emotions are yours. The pain expressed in a scream when you stub a toe. The wail that rises from the soul when a loved one is no longer present (laid to rest). The laughter from hearing an on-point joke that makes your side hurt. The anger that fumes when you've been lied to, on, or about. You have a right to feel the way you do. So do I; that's why I choose to excuse you...

Expressions on Minding Your Own Business

It's Not for You to Know… the struggle of knowing where your next meal's coming from, how you're going to pay the rent, or if you have enough gas in the car to make it to work… a place where you'd rather not be. It's not for you to know the unsolicited pain that comes from racial slurs or the stereotypical false judgment because you happen to be born the way the Lord intended. It is for you to know love, respect, and honor. Most days, those can seem like figments of your imagination. Yet, I've not hidden my scars and muffled the groaning from the sorrow in my soul. Nor did I lie and say you wouldn't discover the challenges that life would bring to you. It's a mother's prayer that wants to protect her young. However, that path I walked was meant for me. The road has been paved. The landmarks have been memorialized.

Now, it's time for you to spread your wings and fly.

Expressions Through a Smile

A **smile** is worth a million words,

But the questions to ask are...

"What is behind that smile?"

"What is in one's mind, heart, spirit, and soul?"

"What are one's fears, goals, and dreams?"

"Does one know how to love?"

"Was one able to receive or give love?"

"What about the voice that speaks through that smile?"

"Is there joy, pain, anger, and/or relief?"

Take a moment to observe.

Ask the questions, or you may never know.

Expressions on Validation

Since when did you need validation?

Wasn't God creating you enough?

Wasn't Him sparing your life enough?

Wasn't Him receiving you enough?

Wasn't His Holy Spirit enough?

Weren't His promises enough?

You don't need a man's approval! Look into His Word! Look in the mirror! You are a reflection, an expressed image of The Divine and Beautiful Creator!

That heartbeat. The twinkle of your eyes. The powerful sound of your voice. The brightness of your smile…

You are validated by the precious blood and righteousness of Jesus Christ! Amen.

Psalm 139:13-17 and 17:8; Isaiah 49:16; Jeremiah 1:5; Exodus 33:12

Expressions on Loyalty

Can you do right by me?

I don't ask for much.

We don't have to see each other every day,

But just keep in touch.

Pay a little compliment If you see me at my best.

Not looking for you to always pay the rent

Because together we can be co-dependent.

Accept me as who I am

In all my ways, And I can do the same,

Hoping for brighter days.

Can you do right by me?

I don't ask for much.

Respect with some TLC, honesty, and trust.

Expressions of Intimacy and Gratitude

(Into - Me - See)

1. Favorite Food: Food... LOL. If I don't have an allergic reaction to it, I'll try it at least once. If I enjoy it, I'll recreate it, adding a few spices to my own liking. Gratitude: Joy

2. Dream Vacation: I'd love to see as much of God's beautiful creation as possible. I now travel intentionally, seeing new places to make my dreams a reality. Gratitude: My Passport

3. Greatest Accomplishment: Learning not to be so hard on myself. Having struggled with perfection and overachieving, accepting imperfections, and wanting a level of excellence in my life is something I can live with. Gratitude: Change

4. Favorite Color(s): Oranges, corals, and rose golds.

   Seeing them accentuate my chocolate skin tone makes me feel pretty. Gratitude: Natural Beauty.

5. Favorite Movie: *Breakfast at Tiffany's* —Audrey Hepburn was phenomenal in that movie! I love, love! Seeing it. Experiencing it. Expressing it. Gratitude: Love

6. The one thing I could live without—pessimism. I naturally see what could be good about people or situations.

Every day brings with it the possibility to do things differently. Gratitude: Forgiveness

7. Employee or entrepreneur? Entrepreneurship, hands down! We must work, so why should our work be based on what others think we're worth? Yet, we must start somewhere. Gratitude: Humility

8. Friend, girlfriend, or wife? Why can't I be all the above—marry, befriend, and date my husband?! Gratitude: Answered Prayers

9. Favorite Music: Smooth jazz—I love instrumentals. Especially the horns! Gratitude: Praise

10. Favorite Scripture: Psalm 24:10—My Heavenly Father keeps His promises. He takes care of me daily! Amen. Gratitude: Provision

11. I don't have to have the last say! I will apologize when I am wrong. My actions will show changed behavior. Gratitude: Repentance

12. Watch TV or Read: Reading is my preference. I have a small library. Education. Inspiration. Self-development. With each page that is bent or statement that is highlighted, I see the area of my life where it could be applied. Gratitude: Progress

13. When I was younger, my Mom told me that I had a wild spirit. I pictured a black stallion running free throughout the land. There was much truth to what she had seen in me. If there were limits, I'd test them. If I were told no, I'd have to find out why. Thank God for the Holy Spirit! Only He could tame me! Sometimes, I

buck, but most times... I yield. Gratitude: Maturity

14. Diamond or Pearls: How about Morganite? It's a beautiful coral, peachy jewel. Set in some rose gold—classy! Gratitude: Uniqueness

15. Knowing who I was, being very much in tune with who I am, and anticipating the woman I date to become is still enough! Gratitude: Value

16. Favorite Song: *It Is Well with My Soul!* I had a nervous breakdown in my early twenties. I was told that I'd have to learn everything all over again. I am a warrior! It's natural for me to fight for a life. It was mine on the line, and I wanted to live! Gratitude: Restoration

17. I've worn fades, Jeri curl, weave, braids, and wigs. Hair is an accessory! It compliments who I am. It doesn't make me who I am! Gratitude: Identity

18. Most recent words shared: "Regardless of what has happened to you, in your life, what are you going to do about it?!" Life has treated you that way for a reason. Again, what are you going to do about it? Gratitude: Accountability

19. From poetry, sketching faces, crocheting blankets, styling hair, sewing masks, to making jewelry, there's pleasure in sharing your gifts with the world. Gratitude: Creativity

20. I know how to live with plenty. I know what it's like to be in need. I have learned the importance of living within my means. There's nothing worse than struggling

to keep what I can't afford. It's also important to know when to let things go. Gratitude: Moderation

21. I am whomever I have to be, to reach at least one. A witness who testifies to the countless attributes of a loving Savior. I love Jesus! Gratitude: Salvation

22. It was frustrating when others couldn't seem to grasp a subject at hand. Yet, I am reminded that I don't always get things. Honestly, there are things that go over my head. Still learning to exercise patience. Gratitude: Understanding

23. Give. Serve. Teach. These are all strengths. Being anxious?! This seems to be a thorn. I've prayed for this to be taken from me. But God! He always strengthens me through teachable moments. Gratitude: Grace

24. Thank you for accompanying me toward the close of another chapter in my life. Much thought was given to the questions and statements that have been shared—in no particular order, but with honesty and transparency. The woman that God has made and is still becoming. Excited about what is still yet to come! Gratitude: Reflections, Blessings, and Hope

25. These 25 Days of Intimacy—Closeness (See into me) were initially shared via IG @nichehodge. This is the last entry: #Chapter 43.

By the time this book is published, I'll be crossing over into #Chapter 45. To God be the glory!

Every day when I wake up, I give God thanks for allowing

me to see life on this side. There are times when I name each blessing, and other times, I am general with my gratitude. However, I am always aware that I and all that are in my possession are gifts, including the time that remains. My life's purpose is to make an impact for the Kingdom of God; love others; and use my gifts, skills, and experiences to share with others the goodness and grace of God. I am unapologetically unashamed of all that God has done for and been to me. It is no longer a burden to carry the light. I will no longer dim the light that radiates from within. Hallelujah! Amen.

A Mother's Love

In Memory of my late Mother, Shirley Hodge

A mother's love cannot be measured by the amount of things she gives to her children that will soon be forgotten.

A mother's love is filled with the sharing of discipline, wisdom, guidance, and strength.

My mother was a strong, and sometimes severe, disciplinarian. My mother was wise about the Word of God, although some may believe her wisdom could've been exercised differently. That I also believe to be true. Yet, I am grateful for the wisdom she has imparted to me.

My mother guided us in silence. A word was not much uttered, but her children knew what they had to do.

My mother guided me in spiritual matters, encouraging me to pray and trust God to keep me in whatever I was going through.

The strength of my mother was never seen in another being that I have ever known. I do not know any time in my mother's life when she didn't have to struggle. However, she passed on a portion of that strength to me.

Almost nothing could break or bend my mother. If she fell, it was on her knees or face to go before God on my behalf or the behalf of others.

She was a mighty woman of valor, a warrior for Christ, not afraid to stand up against the enemy. She knew her victory was already there in whatever test she faced. She also taught me not to give up, but to earnestly seek God, believing that He is more than able to keep the promises He made to us. I knew she was diligent and faithful to the end.

47

Lyrics of a Believer

Est. 4.12.2014

I believe, yes, I believe,
For I can do all things through Christ who strengthens
me.
I believe, yes, I believe.
Nothing is impossible.
I believe.
I am strong, yes, I believe.
I am rich, yes, I believe.
I soar like eagles, yes, I believe.
Over mountains and the sea,
Oh, I believe, yes, I believe.
Yes, Lord, I believe!
You said it. Lord, I believe!
Please help my unbelief!
Please help my unbelief!

The Subject of FACT

Fear

The subject of FACT is FEAR...

Some state that they have FAITH. Yet, when you are the answer to prayer, they reject you and continue asking God for that same help.

"Lord, I need some money!"

The Lord's response: "*I've given you power to get wealth!*" — *Deut. 8:18*

In that truth, with most of God's principles, there is something that has to be done on our part. Yes, we ask, or petition in prayer for the specific need. The next step is to activate or put that faith to work.

When you doubt, you admit your fear and stay stuck, sometimes canceling the prayers and even forfeiting the blessing... Wow!

Fear is a natural reaction of the flesh. Yet, just live and walk by faith, in the power of the Holy Spirit. Hasn't fear of what you possess the power to overcome, and have great victory over, cost you enough?!

"DO IT AFRAID!"

I plan on it! I've got nothing more to lose! When I am weak, I am strong! I can do all that God has given me to do, in His strength! I am victorious! God has not given me the spirit of fear. I have power, strength, and a sound mind! Amen

I declare that I am blessed. All my needs are met. I am debt-free. I have all the money that I will ever need. I have more than enough for myself, my household, and plenty left over to be a blessing to many.

In the name of Jesus! Hallelujah! Amen. Amen. Amen.

Humility

The subject of FACT is HUMILITY.

There are many scriptures that refer to humility, but this one speaks more clearly about what we should do personally.

When you know who God is and His expectations of you and know who you are in Him... there's a sense of pride.

Pride, in which God is not pleased. So much so that His words tell us in 1 Peter 5:6, "*Humble yourselves*" ...

When you believe the Word of God that says you are to be bold and courageous, and that no weapon formed against you shall prosper... those can be foreign to others. Some just don't know, let alone understand.

You know that you are free in Christ Jesus and by the power of the Holy Spirit. Great! You know that all that God made was good, and when it comes to eating what He called good, there are some who object.

The point is your freedom should not cause others to stumble. Be considerate of others. We're not all on the same level! Instead of being arrogant in what we know, let's commit to being more patient with others. That conscious act of humility will go a long way. Amen.

Planning

The subject of FACT is PLANNING.

When you have no sense of direction, how do you know where you're going? If you don't know where you're going, you're bound to follow someone or something.

It's not wise to just pass-through life. Why not make your mark, letting others know that you were here?

Truth be told, you are where you are at this very moment because of the choices you made. Not choosing is still a decision! If you're not pleased about it, what do you plan to do differently?

Take responsibility for the life that you've been given! If you are here, at this moment, you have much to say about what happens next! Amen.

Contentment

The subject of FACT is CONTENTMENT.

We are all consumers!!! Many of us have more than we need. Closets filled with clothing and shoes that we seldom wear. Some items may still have tags on them! We eat more than we should out of gluttony. We'll cling to the old, claiming sentimental value. Yet, out of fear, we don't make room for the new.

While food, clothing, and shelter are the essentials for survival, anything in excess can be an attempt to satisfy an empty place that only God can fill.

It's okay to have nice things, such as a house, car, jewelry, etc.... Sure! Why not enjoy the fruit of your labor?

It's also important to know your motives and attitudes for acquiring or accumulating such things and be careful not to make idols.

Contentment doesn't come easily, but it can be learned. So, let's learn to be content with what we have.

When we are blessed with more, it's an opportunity to practice generosity. For we are only stewards over the things that we have for a time. Amen.

"And having food and clothing, with these we shall be content." — *1 Timothy 6:8*

Believe

The subject of FACT is BELIEVE.

The BIBLE is one of my favorites and most powerful books. It is filled with treasures from history, which are still useful in everyday life. It also contains: Basic Instructions Before Leaving Earth…

So, I've heard. So, I've lived. So, I believe.

As Christians, followers of Jesus Christ, we identify as Believers or disciples. Yet, for a moment, consider this.

Having faith and believing collectively as a body is great. We can believe with our brothers and sisters that things will turn around for the better. When they do, we rejoice with them. However, just as God has given each of us a measure of faith individually, that's how we ought to exercise it, personally.

You read the Bible and believe what it says. The promises about your life, the possibilities, and the potential. Yet, if you fail to do nothing with what you believe, how effective will your life be?!

While others share your faith and pray with you or for you, you must learn to believe that what you're expecting is going to happen. Believing takes courage! It's like you're daring (not testing) God to prove Himself. When He does, it's truly amazing!

Lord, I believe! Help my unbelief! In the name of Jesus!
Amen.

Advocacy

The subject of FACT is ADVOCATE.

God has delivered you to be a witness to others. Don't be afraid to glorify Him with your testimony!

Share with people how Jesus saved you! Jesus advocates through the Holy Spirit and helps you in every area of your life. Tell them that God is a healer, redeemer, protector, provider, counselor, comforter, and all that He still is to you. I believe He allows many to cross our path to brag about who we say we love and serve.

You don't have to be deep. Just be honest! Amen.

Peace and Blessings.

If you are in immediate danger, call 9-1-1.

For anonymous, confidential help, 24/7, please call the National Domestic Violence Hotline at 1-800-799-7233 (SAFE) or 1-800-787-3224 (TTY).

Responsibility

The subject of FACT is RESPONSIBILITY.

As a born citizen of the United States of America, it is my RESPONSIBILITY to exercise my civil rights!

As a blood-bought believer, citizen of the Kingdom of God, it is my RESPONSIBILITY to honor God by taking the stewardship He has given to me seriously!

As a woman, daughter, mother, sister, and friend, it is my RESPONSIBILITY to listen, love, and lead in acts of service in my home, community, and country. Amen.

The subject of FACT is RESPONSIBILITY.

Love

The subject of FACT is LOVE.

I can discuss this four-letter word in many different ways. Today is about personal responsibility. Remember, it always begins with **YOU**! Amen.

Matthew 22:39b – "Love **YOU**r neighbor as **YOU**rSELF."

I can only love anyone to the extent or measure that I love myself.

I am beautiful, smart, intelligent, fair, considerate, kind, compassionate, trustworthy, faithful, and lovable... Since I know that and more about myself, I don't need anyone to tell me those things.

You can say, "I'm full of myself!" and I would definitely agree. It's easy for me to love! However, I am more careful of not allowing others to abuse my love or take it for granted. Love is an action word and has little to do with emotions. I "feel" a way throughout the day, depending on the subject at hand. Yet, out of love, I do what is necessary to make life simpler for myself and others... even when I don't feel like it!

Amen.

I love you! Not because you love me, but because I love me.

Thoughts—Thinking

The subject of FACT is THOUGHTS/THINKING.

This can also be discussed in greater detail.

Our thoughts are created in our mind, which the Bible also calls our heart. Our heart holds on to ideas and emotions, which will eventually produce actions.

Thoughts are very important. The result of them determines how we live, or even the quality of our lives.

A favorite verse on the subject is Proverbs 23:7 NKJV—"For as he THINKS in his heart, so is he…"

I believe what God says about me, so I take the time to learn about how He thinks and of the promises made to me.

Each day, with the help of the Holy Spirit, I can start fresh, strengthening areas of my life that may lack the resemblance of the thoughts or promises of God.

The Bible also shares this about our thoughts—they are inherently evil. They reveal who we are and how we can change the ways in which we think. Most importantly, we are reminded of the sovereignty of Almighty God, that He and His ways are greater than we could ever think or imagine. Hallelujah! Amen.

If you think that what you're thinking doesn't matter, think again. Amen.

Isolation—Solitude

The subject of FACT is ISOLATION/SOLITUDE.

What is your first reaction when you are in a period or season of isolation? Do you reach for the radio, or the remote? Do you use those times for cleansing and reflection? Do you rest, or rush to more distraction?

There are times when life causes us to be alone, and isolation makes us feel lonely. No calls or visitors. We try to reach for anyone, but no one responds. We have our thoughts and may even hear the sound of the wind whistling, the fridge silently humming, or a clock ticking on the wall.

This year, 2020, will be remembered! Pandemic. Crisis. Death by the masses. We were sent home from school, work, church, and play. We were distanced from some family, friends, and peers. We cried, prayed, questioned, and ultimately stood firm in our faith.

It appears time slowed down just enough for us to get to know each other again, or reveal that we were really

strangers after all. In forced isolation, we chose to grow closer or drift further apart. It caused us to make tough decisions while remembering our values, vows, and what matters most. Love. Forgiveness. Reconciliation. Support. Kindness. Mercy. Sacrifice.

If God hasn't gotten your attention by now, He will

do whatever it takes to get it! His words created our existence, and His works are evident throughout all time. He will move everything from your life so that you only seek and see Him. Dare to ask what else could happen? He is sovereign enough to show you!

Let's go, voluntarily, away from the noise, into a quiet place, with a humble posture of complete surrender. For when we sense no one by our side, He is always there, ready to answer. Amen.

Limitations

The subject of FACT is LIMITATIONS.

I can do all things through Christ who strengthens me...

Sure. You can do all the things that you desire to do. You may even do them well. Yet just because an invitation has been extended to help in some area, it doesn't mean that you should.

There have been times when we have taken action just because we thought someone should. The results were disappointing or even disastrous. Why? What was the goal? What about intentions or motives?

Can you really do all of that? That which you said you could? Volunteered to do? Willed yourself to do? Are you gifted in that area? Will all of what you choose to do add value to those around you?

It's not a question of your ability or trying to prove a point that it can be done. It's about maximizing, operating, and succeeding in your own gift(s) to the benefit of others.

The fact is, we all have limitations! No one is exempt. It's a sign of growth and maturity, accepting the fact that we cannot do everything! And that's okay! Amen.

Vulnerable

The subject of **FACT** is: VULNERABLE.

Being vulnerable is scary! Yet, if you're always guarded, how can anyone get to you, or how do you expect much more to pass through you?

Now, plenty of good has come from pain. Salvation is a major factor. Jesus was vulnerable and prayed for that cup to pass. Nevertheless, by His obedience to His Father, He went to the cross in our place. Hallelujah! Amen!

The FACT is, we shouldn't allow our vulnerability to cause us to think that we are weak, afraid, or invaluable—to paralyze us from moving forward in life. That opportunity may not pass your way again.

Love them now. Apologize while they're alive. Say yes to that new job. Whatever is staring you in the face—look back at, and deal with it!!!

Be strong and of good courage! Love with passion in truth! Most importantly, receive that answered prayer without questioning your worth.

Exchange

The subject of FACT is EXCHANGE.

Assurance costs.

Believing costs.

Career costs.

Destiny costs.

Education costs.

Freedom costs.

Greatness costs.

Humility costs.

Independence costs.

Justice costs.

Kindness costs. Love costs.

Maturity costs

Necessity costs.

Optimism costs.

Pleasure costs.

Quitting costs.

Reasoning costs.

Sacrifices costs.

Truth costs.

Understanding costs.

Value costs.

Excuses cost.

Yielding costs.

Wisdom costs. Zest costs.

By now, you've gotten the picture.

The FACT is, all that you want, or desire requires something for it. The question is... What are you willing to give in EXCHANGE for it? Be careful how you choose! Amen.

I Found My Voice

As a young girl, I prayed, believing that God would hear me. Yet, as I grew, the enemy tried everything to silence me… But the prayers of my Mommy and others, including the intercession of Jesus Himself, helped to restore my voice.

It wasn't until my Mom passed that God began to deal with me again about prayer. I was reminded to give God back His Word and remind Him of the promises that He made to me. That it wasn't my name or reputation on the line… Oh, Lord, it is to You I cry! For Your name's sake, hasten Your Word to perform it!

He said that He already knew the words before they'd form on my tongue. He just wanted to hear them. Raw. Real. Simple. I didn't have to rehearse what I'd say, but as I felt it, I'd pour my heart out to Him.

Now throughout my day, as I hear in the ear or see via text, I pray. A simple prayer. Straight to the issue. Being respectful. Being firm. Being grateful. Waiting with expectancy.
Acknowledging His presence and ability to resolve… but humble enough to still come as I am, and leave changed… even if there's no immediate change of my situation. What a relief!

At times when it may seem as though I don't have much to give, I can offer a prayer.

Dear Lord,
I am so glad that while I am yet praying, You hear.
I believe it will all be done according to Your divine will
and perfect plan. Thank You that You are merciful, in
spite of me. In the name of Jesus. Amen.

I Am Growing – Not Grown

Despite ALLLLLLL my issues, God loves me the same. He is NOT like man, who changes like the weather. God IS the same as He was yesterday and today, and He WILL be the same forever.

I'm Growing day by day.

I'm Relying on God more instead of myself and other people. I'm Owning up to the responsibilities that I have and not passing them onto others.

I'm Working on my attitudes, insecurities, and issues...

I'm Not going to be too hard on myself when something I want to work out doesn't.

I can't always have my way!

(smile)

Open Doors

Listen. Can you hear that? What is that sound? At times, it is persistent and loud. Other times, it is vague and distant. Yet, I am certain that I recognize the sound of knocking...

Each day, many doors are opened for you, and you must choose if you are going to walk around them, past them, or through them. Doors are considered opportunities. The first door you see when you get up is life. By the grace of God and His brand-new mercy, you are above ground, breathing, and living. The second door is touched when your feet hit the ground. Then, there is the door of decision. You decide whether your day will be good and positive or negative and bad by the attitude you have and the confessions you make. The next door is what you walk out of to face the world, and if you work at home, then that is the door in which you walk through to start the many activities of your day.

Here is a powerful scripture that speaks to us about open doors and liberty. The message is shared after there was a false accusation and imprisonment. Instead of retaliation, there was praise and worship. Although the men involved were physically bound, their minds and hearts were not. Knowing that their spirits were free and in one accord, they acted positively despite a negative situation, and that brought about a great change.

Acts 16:26: *"Suddenly, there was a great earthquake, so that the foundations of the prison were shaken; and immediately all the doors were opened, and everyone's chains were loosed."*

What in your life must be shaken for you to make a change? What doors are open that you are afraid to walk through? Which doors in your life do you have to close, throw away the key, and possibly move to a new address to leave alone? What is keeping you chained and in bondage? The questions asked are for you to take an honest evaluation of your life. The things that are or are not taking place now are responses to decisions that you have made or failed to make. What are you going to do now?

Have you taken time out to greet someone or offer to hold the door or elevator for someone? There is the door to humility and kindness.

Did you review the drafted letter or memo before sending it out to your staff or clients? There is another door to careful attention and consideration.

Will you return the call as promised, even though your schedule is already tight? There is yet one more door that leads to trustworthiness and reliability.

We are exposed to many doors daily. It is our decisions that can make a great impact on the lives around us. Today is the first day of autumn or fall. Let this message resonate with you, and as you are crossing over the threshold of the open doors in your lives, leave the anger, bitterness, envy, fear, gossip, hate, negativity, poisonous attitudes, and behavior outside.

Be blessed and have a colorful and passionate new season!

On Purpose

Most of the time, we know what we are going to do. We do this by having a plan, preferably written down, that we can visit often to make sure that we are on track. When something doesn't seem to line up, we make the necessary adjustments to steer us back in the right direction.

Today, I would like to discuss the words, "On Purpose." This is a simple, yet profound phrase that has a different meaning to each of us. For me, when I am given a word, I like to see what God has to say about it in His Word. The scripture reference that stands out is Romans 8:28, and it isn't really talking about what we purpose for ourselves, but the purpose of God in our lives.

"And we know that all things work together for good to those who love God, to those who are the called according to His purpose."

There are good days, bad days, some regrets, and great expectations that we experience at one time or another. At times, during tests or trials, we cannot understand why we are going through them. Most likely, we have not the slightest clue as to why 'this' is happening. As we see above, it is for God's purposes because anything at all occurs. He is not a respecter of persons, and He doesn't show favoritism. He also doesn't have to explain or answer why when we ask. This can be frustrating. However, life, as it happens, will teach us many things if we are willing to learn.

What do we do when we need an answer about
something that has been pressing so hard on us that it
seems as though we can't breathe? Pray. We should
open our mouths and cry out, "HELP!" Believe me, God
hears and will answer. Let's try to remember that God
doesn't do things the way we do. We can't afford to miss
out on a breakthrough because deliverance didn't come
the way that we hoped or wanted it to. Just say, "Thank
you," for receiving the help that you prayed for.

Once we've prayed, and there is still a delay in 'that'
answer, we ought to position ourselves for 'the' answer.
For example, you have been seeking a job, but you don't
have a suit that you can go to an interview in. How do
you proceed? If you're humble enough, you can ask a
friend to lend you one, or you can visit a thrift store to
purchase a suit for less than $12. Don't allow pride to
block your blessing! Another idea is that when you have
time to lend to others, try volunteering at an organization
that you are passionate about. When you learn about
why they do what they do, you will more than likely
discover more about yourself. This is simply working
while you wait. Also, it is a good thing to share with the
group what skills you would hope to gain, as well. The
process you take doesn't have to be extreme. It can be
one that you are sure about and that will help guide you
further in the direction you are going.

Finally, once you have prayed and positioned yourself
to receive an answer, you should practice having an
attitude of gratitude, offer a shout of praise, and even
do a victory dance. You don't have to wait until the test
is over to give a testimony. You can reflect on what you
have already overcome and try your best to remember

that the same God who did miracles for you and on your half before is still the same God. His promises haven't changed! His power hasn't changed! Certainly, His position hasn't changed!

Out of ALL that you have been through... admit that you didn't think you'd make it, but by the grace of God, you're still here! Why? To be a witness for God that He saves, heals, and delivers! Your life is to glorify Him! So, the next time the thunder roars, the heavens flood down rain, and the violent wind blows, shredding some leaves off the trees in your yard, thank God that He has on purpose, a master plan that is all working together for your good. Amen.

It Takes All That

Why do you do what you do? Is it to satisfy the longing desire within you, or is it to save face by constantly trying to please someone who could care less about you or your future? Are you living your dreams, or are you preoccupied with making others a reality that you don't even know your own purpose?

This message is shared to encourage all of us to stop listening to people who tell us that we can't do what we know in our hearts we can do. I heard the other day, "Do it afraid..." The profound statement spoke volumes of the truth that regardless of how you are doing it, you're doing it!

You're a dedicated fan who has purchased season tickets for your favorite college football team every year since 1996. Why do it? You love sports and coaching your child's team. You're committed to being bilingual, so you travel frequently to Spain, Brazil, and Puerto Rico to learn more about the different dialects of the Spanish language. You've even decided to relocate for a job that would require you to speak the native language daily. Why travel that far?

You want to touch as many lives as you can.

You're studying for that professional certification, which means less time for social media. What, you're not on Facebook or Twitter? Nope! Why? The time I'm investing now means that I can have more financial freedom later.

If you had to be honest, haven't you put enough time and energy into some things that you don't even remember, let alone some things that were of value? Whatever has your attention, if it's going to enhance you being a greater asset, add to your joy and peace of mind, or set you above the standard; why not do it with all that is within you?

ECCLESIASTES 9:10 (emphasis added, multiple translations)

AMP - *Whatever your hand finds to do, do it with all your might...*
CEB - *Whatever you are capable of doing, do with all your might...*
CEV - *Work hard at whatever you do...*
TLB - *Whatever you do, do well...*
NABRE - *Anything you can turn your hand to, do with what power you have...*
NCV - *Whatever work you do, do your best...*
NVL - *Whatever your hand finds to do, do it with all your strength...*

So, from this point on, if it means long hours at the gym, dual enrollment in high school or double major in college, volunteering at the local shelter, being a companion to your elderly neighbor, worshiping at church until you sweat or praising until you've lost your voice, dating for two-plus years to make sure that is the person you don't want to live without, standing in line to get the newest phone out there... Do it! And should someone have the unmitigated audacity to say to you, "It don't take all that!" ... If you even care to respond, you can boldly reply, "YES, IT DOES! And I'm going to do whatever it takes!"

Answered Prayers

I can gratefully say that I live a life of answered prayers. From spiritual growth, healthy relationships, career, and traveling to see much of God's beautiful creation, the Lord has heard and answered specific prayers.

Prayer for Healthy Relationships

Heavenly Father,

I thank You for answering prayers! For placing women, godly women, and role models into my life. Thank You that we can encourage, uplift, care for, pray with and for, stand with, and love one another. Abundantly bless the women whom You placed in my life, in various seasons, and for different reasons, who have become sisters, cousins, aunts, and spiritual mentors... Meet them, this day, at their greatest point of need. Comfort them. Place Your loving arms around them and hold them close. For every tear they cry, give them joy and laughter. Exchange the heavy burdens they carry with Your grace and peace. Let Your mighty strength be made perfect in all their weaknesses.

Help us to be faithful to You and to one another. Help us to speak the truth in love, instead of gossiping about one another. Help us to forgive when we are offended.

Help us to leave vengeance to You when others lie on us, manipulate us, cheat us, or even curse us. Help us to pray for one another, trusting You to work things out as You see fit. Help us to love You. Teach us to love ourselves so we can truly love others...

Lord, please save my friends. Heal them. Deliver them.

Protect them. Help them to be in right standing with You.

Thank You for hearing and answering this prayer for my friends. I seal this prayer with the precious blood of Jesus and the fire of the Holy Spirit. In Jesus's name, AMEN!

Remember Me

It was after the death of my mother that I really began to think about life. What was the purpose? Whose life will be encouraged by the one I chose to live? Perhaps, the most important thing to consider: What kind of legacy would I leave?

Maya Angelou once said, "Legacy is every life you touch." While that is true, as a believer, the impact I hope to make is that of God's kingdom.

Did I: give, love, forgive, show compassion, meet a need, listen to a hurting heart, pray for those who love and hate me, and/or pour my life out as an offering so that God would be glorified? I pray that I have!

Now, I'm sure there were plenty of times when I missed the mark because I was blind, hard-headed and/or hard-hearted, stubborn, or just living a rebellious life. Thank God for Jesus! For redemption! For changing my heart and mind, drawing me back to Him! Amen!

An earnest prayer is to hear, "Well done!"

Until then, I have committed, for the rest of my days, to live holy, pure, and righteous, simply because that is who God is!

Will there be temptations? Absolutely! Will I give in? I'm certain! However, I acknowledge that this Christian journey has not, nor will ever, be easy or without challenges, trials, or tribulations.

But God!

He is faithful to keep me! I want to be kept! My desire is

to please Him more than I please mankind. It's a conscious decision to submit my will to His daily, being completely honest when I just don't want to do what He said. Amen.

So, if today was my last day, these would be my parting words:

"I have lived intentionally. I laughed on purpose… a lot… but most importantly, I have loved with the ability in which I was able!

While your emotions may be cloudy, may the love of Jesus comfort your hearts and clear your mind, bringing you joy and peace.

Don't hold onto any bitterness or anger. Also, release resentment and pride. Humble yourself before the Lord, who will lift you up in due time.

Remember, to know God, you will know peace, and without Him (JESUS), there is no real, lasting peace.

To everything, there is a season. A time to live and a time to die. Your pain, sorrow, and feelings of uncertainty are temporary. This, too, shall pass! What is certain: GOD IS FAITHFUL TO HIS WORD TO PERFORM IT! Amen."

Peace and Blessings.

Thank you for gracing my life with all that you have been.

Thank you for the opportunity to serve!

About the Author

Nichelle is an Ambassador, Advocate, Author, Artist, and Accountant. A Kingdom Single, who maximizes all the gifts and opportunities that God has bestowed upon her to bless others and make an impact for His Kingdom.

She is a facilitator and learner of the Holy Bible. She enjoys traveling, cooking, crocheting, and most things that celebrate art and culture. You will find her sharing her gifts with those she encounters.

She is committed to a life of service and is available for speaking engagements and to facilitate small group classes that encourage the growth of women in the Kingdom, body of Christ.

NAH II Enterprises, LLC
Lithonia - Stonecrest, GA www.nichehodge.com

Dating without Discrimination

BY NICHELLE HODGE

NICHELLE HODGE

NO LONGER A ~~VICTIM~~

Awareness of Abuse
and
Mental Health